MW01169235

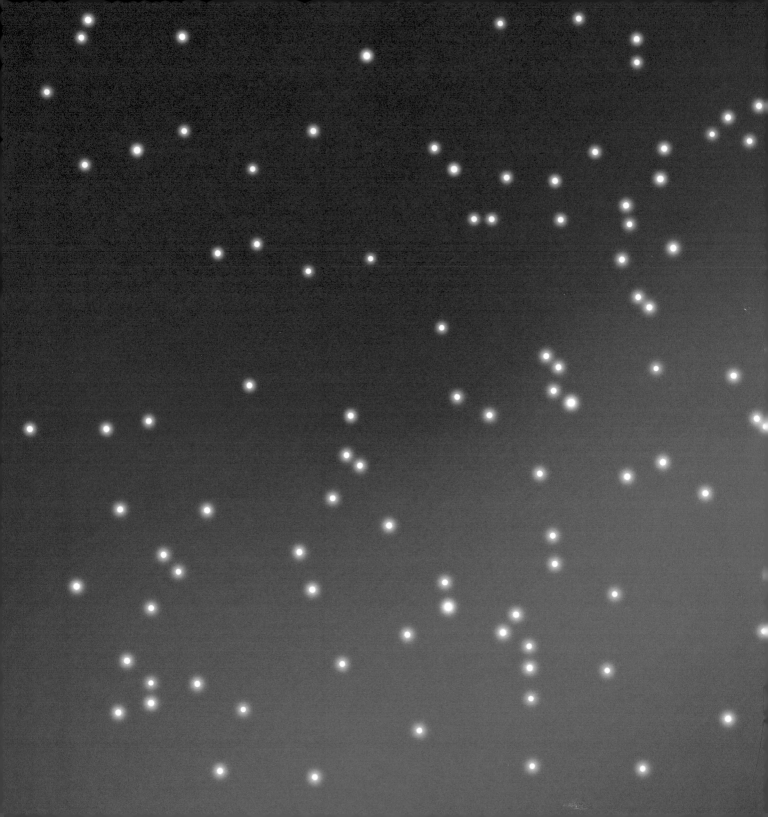

The Quest Cousins Go Camping

Written by Chad Sanders
Illustrated by Sumitra Lokras

The Quest Cousins Go Camping
By Chad Sanders
ISBN : 979-8-9916041-3-0

Follow him on Instagram : @chadsand

Children's Book

First Edition

Cover and Illustrations by Sumitra Lokras (www.illustrationsbysumitra.com)

For Fox,
Cal and
Miles

This book belongs to

Two little cousins
ran into the woods,
Bumbling and stumbling
as fast as they could.

The first thing they did
was go on a hike
To look for the animals
Each of them liked.

Out popped a Fox,
And a deer and a frog.
"Woof, Woof!"said Echo,
Their little puppy dog.

They saw falcons, and turtles
and bears on two feet.
Then Baby Boy said,
"Let's find something to eat."

So the cousins went fishing,
And picked fruit from a tree.
They said, "Thank you forest,
For feeding us three!"

Now their bellies were full,
They were feeling content.
But it started to rain!
So they pitched a big tent.

When the rain was all over,
The cousins popped out,
And noticed a rainbow
replacing the clouds.

But the sun went down, And
the cousins were cold,
Baby Girl had a plan.
It was smart. It was bold.

"Before it gets late,
And we all get too tired,
Let's work together
To make a bonfire!"

The cousins made s'mores
So gooey and sweet,
They made shadow puppets
With their hands and their feet.

The moon came up,
And moon light shined out,
Suddenly there were magical critters about.

The Snakes said HISSSS
The Owls said WHOOO
There were skunks and rabbits,
And bats and raccoons.

Echo ran to the lake,
And let out a "BARK!"
There were jellyfish down there,
that glowed in the dark.

The fireflies flickered,
And danced in the sky,
The cousins jumped into the animal vibe.

They slithered like snakes,
They flapped like the owls,
They danced like the fireflies,
But then came a HOWL!
AROOOOOOOOOOOOOOOOOOOOOOOO!!!!

Somewhere not too far,
A wolf howled at the moon.
The cousins looked at Echo
and what did she do?

AROOOOOOOOOOOOOOOOOOOOOOO!!!!

Echo howled right back!
So the cousins did too!

AROOOOOOOOOOOOOOOOOOOOOOO!!!!

Out there in the woods,
The cousins were free,
Away from the noise,
And from technology.

When the sun came back up,
It was time to go home.
The cousins missed their parents,
And Echo missed her bone.

The cousins hugged the animals,
And the bugs and the trees,
And they said, "Thank you, forest,
For letting us be free."

Made in United States
Troutdale, OR
11/07/2024

24440894R00017